Cello Time Runners

a second book of easy pieces for cello

Kathy and David Blackwell

illustrations by Alan Rowe

Grateful thanks are due to Polly Chilcott, Alison Ingram, Avril Ivin, Tom Morter, and Janet Parsons for all their help with this volume.

Welcome to **Cello Time Runners**. You'll find:

- pieces using 2nd finger
- pieces using backward and forward extensions
- semiquavers, dotted crotchets, and 6/8 time
- a new piece, replacing no. 8
- duets, with parts of equal difficulty
- scales and arpeggios covering the keys you'll find in the book, plus G major 2 octaves
- Music Fact-Finder Pages at the back to help explain words and signs
- play-along tracks available to download from **www.oup.com/ctrunners2e** or to stream on major streaming platforms. Pieces counted in; drumkit added for the jazz and rock numbers
- straightforward piano accompaniments available in a separate volume

OXFORD
UNIVERSITY PRESS

1. Start the show

(for Clare)

KB & DB

Count 4 bars

Rock tempo

OXFORD UNIVERSITY PRESS, MUSIC DEPARTMENT, GREAT CLARENDON STREET, OXFORD OX2 6DP

2. Banyan tree

Jamaican folk tune

3. Heat haze

KB & DB

4. Medieval tale

KB & DB

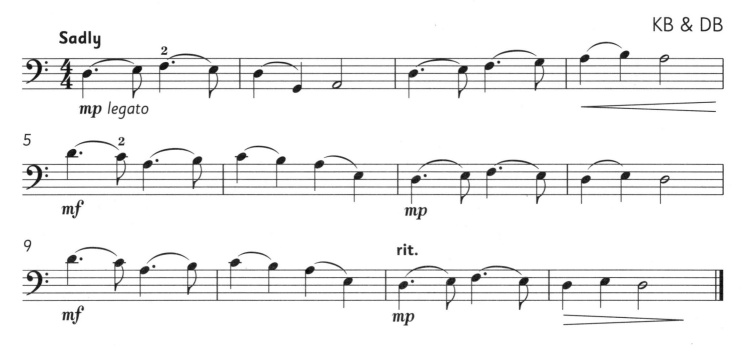

5. Chase in the dark

5

6. Spy movie

KB & DB

7. Romani band

KB & DB

8. Busy day

KB & DB

9. On the go!

10. That's how it goes!

KB & DB

Luckily this piece is not as hard as it looks!

11. Blue whale

KB & DB

12. Mean street chase

KB & DB

10

13. Allegretto

Mozart

14. Cornish May song

Cornish folk tune

15. Noël

Daquin

16. Prelude from 'Te Deum'

Charpentier

17. Paris café

18. Starry night

KB & DB

19. Cello Time rag

20. Caribbean sunshine

KB & DB

21. Jacob's dance

KB & DB

22. Song from the show

KB & DB

23. The road to Donegal

KB & DB

Can also be bowed: ♩ ♪ ♩ ♪ | etc.

24. Cat's eyes

25. Mexican fiesta

KB & DB

Use these words to help with the rhythm:

Tro - pi - cal heat-wave in Mex - i - co

26. Summer evening

KB & DB

27. Extension rock

KB & DB

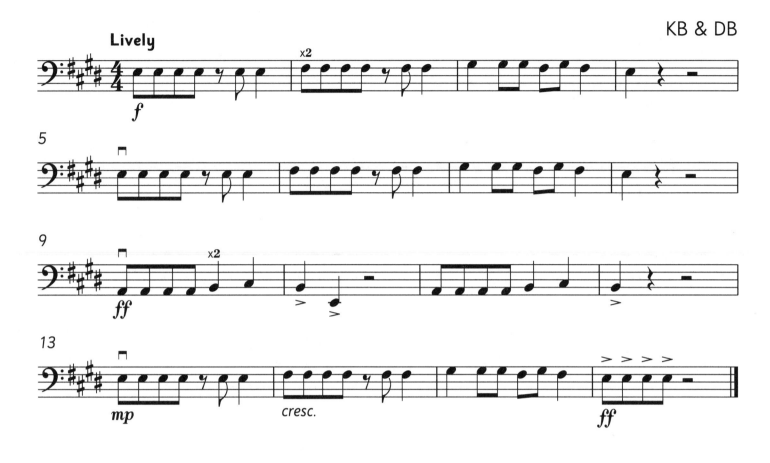

28. Show off!

KB & DB

29. You and me

KB & DB

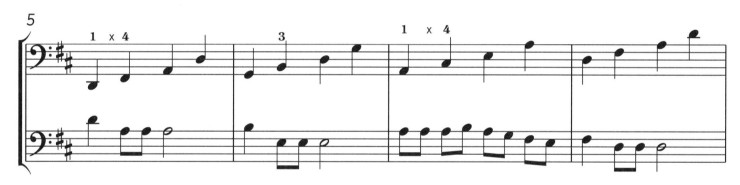

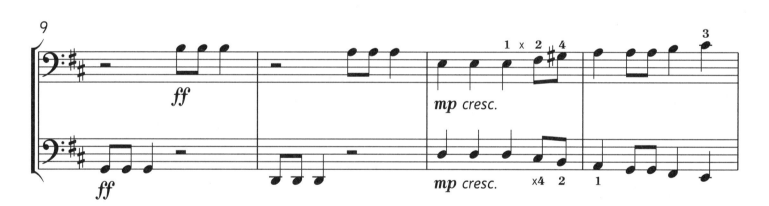

You and me!

30. One day

KB & DB

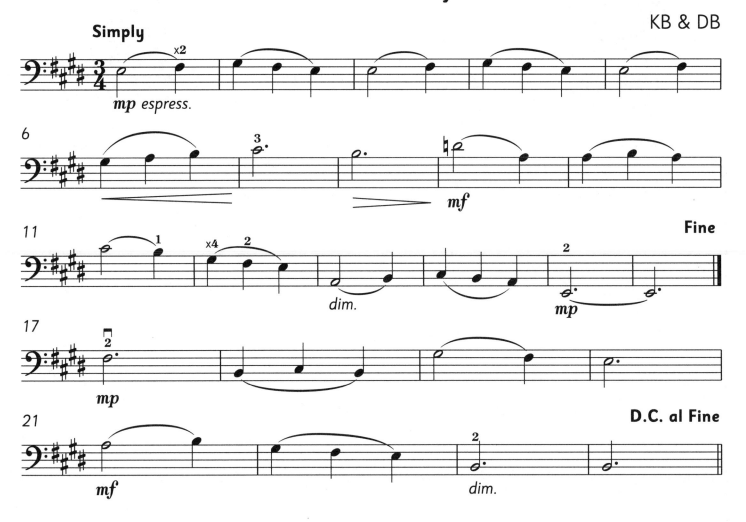

31. Aerobics

KB & DB

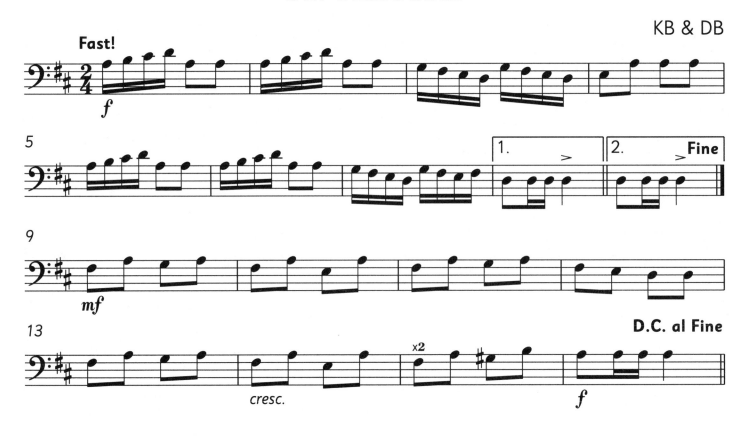

32. Hungarian folk dance

KB & DB

33. Show stopper

KB & DB

34. Farewell to Skye

(for Iain)

KB & DB

Scaley Things

C major scale 2 octaves

C major arpeggio 2 octaves

F major scale 1 octave

F major arpeggio 1 octave

B♭ major scale 1 octave

B♭ major arpeggio 1 octave

D major scale 2 octaves

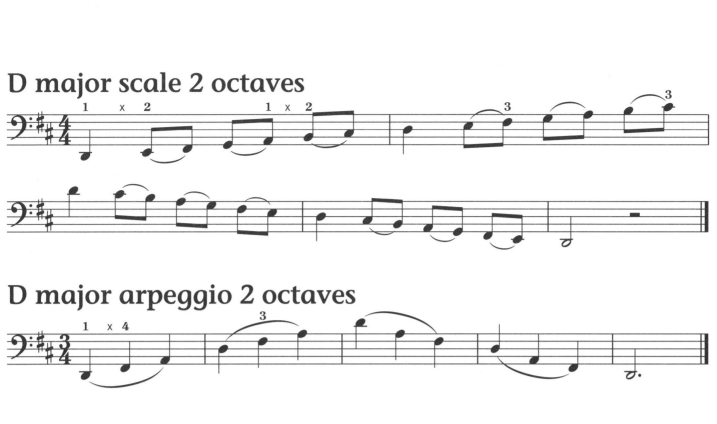

D major arpeggio 2 octaves

A major scale 1 octave

A major arpeggio 1 octave

G harmonic minor scale 1 octave

G melodic minor scale 1 octave

G minor arpeggio 1 octave

D harmonic minor scale 1 octave

D melodic minor scale 1 octave

D minor arpeggio 1 octave

C harmonic minor scale 1 octave

C melodic minor scale 1 octave

C minor arpeggio 1 octave

G major scale 2 octaves

G major arpeggio 2 octaves

Music Fact-Finder Pages

Here are some of the words and signs you will find in some of your pieces!

How to play it

pizzicato or pizz. = pluck

arco = with the bow

⊓ = down bow

V = up bow

> = accent

gliss. (glissando) = slide your finger along the string

Don't get lost!

‖: :‖ = repeat marks

⌐1. ⌐2. = first and second time bars

Play the first bar first time through; skip to the second bar on the repeat

D.C. al Fine = repeat from the beginning and stop at **Fine**

D.℠. al Fine = repeat from the sign ℠ and stop at **Fine**

rit. or **rall.** = gradually getting slower

molto rall. = slow down a lot

a tempo = back to the first speed

⌢ = pause

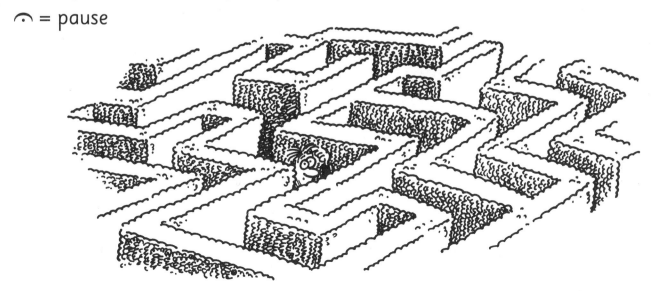

Volume control

p (*piano*) = quiet

mp (*mezzo-piano*) = moderately quiet

mf (*mezzo-forte*) = moderately loud

f (*forte*) = loud

ff (*fortissimo*) = very loud

———————————————— or *crescendo* (*cresc.*)

= getting gradually louder

———————————————— or *diminuendo* (*dim.*)

= getting gradually quieter

Italian phrase-book

accelerando = gradually get faster

Allegro = fast and lively

Allegretto = not too fast

Andante = at a walking pace

espress. = expressively

legato = smoothly

Maestoso = majestically

Moderato = at a moderate speed

staccato = short

Practissimo = lots of Cello Time!

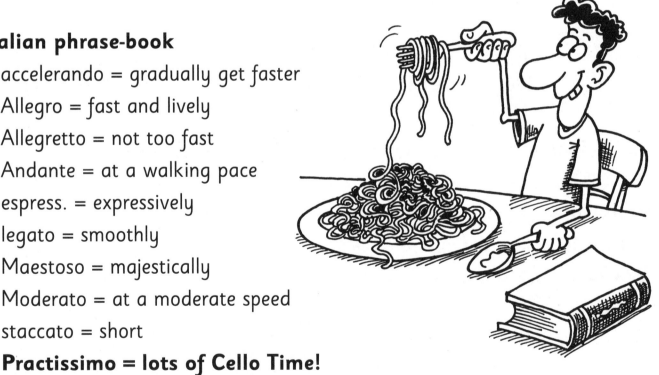